HOW TO DRAW CARTOON CHARACTERS
A BEGINNER'S
ACTIVITY BOOK

JUPITER KIDS

JUPITER KIDS
CHILDREN'S & KIDS FICTION

INSTRUCTIONS FOR DRAWING:

THIS HOW-TO DRAWING BOOK CONSISTS OF IMAGES THAT ARE PLACED ON GRIDS. THERE IS A DRAWING BOX LOCATED AT THE LOWER PART OF THE PAGE AND THAT WILL SERVE AS YOUR PRACTICE SPACE. TO COPY THE IMAGE, DRAW PARTS OF THE IMAGE PER GRID AND PUT THEM ON THE BIGGER GRIDS. SOUNDS DIFFICULT? NOT REALLY. TRY IT FIRST!

IT'S OKAY IF YOU DON'T COPY THE IMAGE PERFECTLY. AFTER ALL, DRAWING IS ABOUT THE EXPRESSION OF YOUR PERCEPTION AS WELL AS YOUR HAND STRENGTH AND CONTROL.

WHEN YOU'VE COPIED THE IMAGE, GO AND AHEAD AND COLOR IT NEXT! WE'RE EXCITED TO SEE WHAT YOU CAN DO!

DRAW
THE
IMAGE

DRAW
THE
IMAGE

DRAW
THE
IMAGE

DRAW
THE
IMAGE

DRAW
THE
IMAGE

DRAW
THE
IMAGE

DRAW
THE
IMAGE

DRAW
THE
IMAGE

DRAW
THE
IMAGE

DRAW
THE
IMAGE

DRAW
THE
IMAGE

DRAW
THE
IMAGE

DRAW
THE
IMAGE

DRAW
THE
IMAGE

DRAW
THE
IMAGE

DRAW
THE
IMAGE

DRAW
THE
IMAGE

DRAW
THE
IMAGE

DRAW
THE
IMAGE

DRAW
THE
IMAGE

DRAW
THE
IMAGE

DRAW
THE
IMAGE

DRAW
THE
IMAGE

DRAW
THE
IMAGE

DRAW
THE
IMAGE

DRAW
THE
IMAGE

DRAW
THE
IMAGE

DRAW
THE
IMAGE

DRAW
THE
IMAGE

DRAW
THE
IMAGE

DRAW
THE
IMAGE

DRAW
THE
IMAGE

DRAW
THE
IMAGE

DRAW
THE
IMAGE

DRAW
THE
IMAGE

DRAW
THE
IMAGE

DRAW
THE
IMAGE

DRAW
THE
IMAGE

DRAW
THE
IMAGE

DRAW
THE
IMAGE

DRAW
THE
IMAGE

DRAW
THE
IMAGE

DRAW
THE
IMAGE

DRAW
THE
IMAGE

DRAW
THE
IMAGE

DRAW
THE
IMAGE

DRAW
THE
IMAGE

DRAW
THE
IMAGE

DRAW
THE
IMAGE

DRAW
THE
IMAGE

DRAW
THE
IMAGE

DRAW
THE
IMAGE

CPSIA information can be obtained
at www.ICGtesting.com
Printed in the USA
BVHW011222080922
646451BV00004B/338